Help the Environment

Caring for Nature

Charlotte Guillain

www.heinemannlibrary.co.uk
Visit our website to find out more information about Heinemann Library books.

To order:
☎ Phone 44 (0) 1865 888066
📄 Send a fax to 44 (0) 1865 314091
💻 Visit the Heinemann Bookshop at www.heinemannlibrary.co.uk to browse our catalogue and order online.

Heinemann Library is an imprint of Capstone Global Library Limited, a company incorporated in England and Wales having its registered office at 7 Pilgrim Street, London, EC4V 6LB – Registered company number: 6695582

Heinemann is a registered trademark of Pearson Education Limited, under licence to Capstone Global Library Limited

Text © Capstone Global Library Limited 2008
First published in hardback in 2008
Paperback edition first published in 2009

Editorial: Sian Smith and Cassie Mayer
Design: Philippa Jenkins
Picture research: Erica Martin, Hannah Taylor and Ginny Stroud-Lewis
Production: Duncan Gilbert

Printed and bound in China by South China Printing Co. Ltd.

ISBN 978 0 431 19220 8 (hardback)
12 11 10 09 08
10 9 8 7 6 5 4 3 2 1

ISBN 978 0 431 19226 0 (paperback)
13 12 11 10 09
10 9 8 7 6 5 4 3 2 1

British Library Cataloguing in Publication Data
Guillain, Charlotte
  Caring for nature. - (Help the environment) (Acorn)
  1. Nature conservation - Juvenile literature
  I. Title
  333.9'516

Acknowledgements
The publishers would like to thank the following for permission to reproduce photographs: ©Alamy pp. **13** (Carlos Davila), **23 middle** (ilian), **4 bottom left** (Kevin Foy), **20** (B. Mete Uz), **19** (Brandon Cole Marine Photography), **17** (Jim West), **4 top right**, **23 top** (Westend 61); ©ardea.com pp. **12**, **23b** (George Reszeter), **10** (Paul Van Gaalen); ©Brand X Pictures p. **4 bottom right** (Morey Milbradt); ©Corbis p. **11** (Simon Marcus); ©Digital Vision p. **4 top left**; ©naturepl.com p. **6** (Aflo); ©Photoeditinc. p. **5** (Michael Newman); ©Photolibrary pp. **15** (Animals Animals, Earth Scenes), **22** (Digital Vision), **21** (Image Source Limited), **14** (Juniors Bildarchiv), **16**, **18** (Mark Hamblin), **7** (Photodisc), **9** (Rodger Jackman), **8** (Stephen Shepherd)

Cover photograph of a butterfly on a flower reproduced with permission of ©Getty Images (Taxi, David McGlynn). Back cover photograph of a boy looking at a stag beetle reproduced with permission of ©Alamy (B. Mete Uz).

Every effort has been made to contact copyright holders of any material reproduced in this book. Any omissions will be rectified in subsequent printings if notice is given to the publishers.

Contents

What is the environment?

The environment is the world
all around us.

We need to care for
the environment.

Who lives in the environment?

Plants and animals live in
the environment.

We need to care for plants
and animals.

Ways to help the environment

Bees need wild flowers.

If we do not pick wild flowers,
we help bees.
We are helping the environment.

Butterflies need wild flowers.

If we do not pick wild flowers,
we help butterflies.
We are helping the environment.

Birds lay eggs in nests.

If we do not touch nests,
we help birds.
We are helping the environment.

13

Birds need water to drink and wash.

When we put water in our garden, we help birds.
We are helping the environment.

Litter can hurt animals.

When we pick up litter,
we help animals.
We are helping the environment.

Wild animals need to be left alone.

If we do not feed wild animals,
we help them.
We are helping the environment.

We can care for nature.

We can help the environment.

How are they helping?

How are these children caring for nature?

Answer on p. 24

Picture glossary

environment the world around us

litter things we do not need any more

nature plants, animals, and other things in the world that are not made by people

Index

Answer to question on p.22: The children are picking up litter. This will stop animals from being hurt by it.

Note to Parents and Teachers

Before reading

Talk to the children about plants and animals in the environment. Have they seen wild flowers growing? Have they seen a wild animal like a squirrel or a fox?

After reading

- Make a waxed paper butterfly ornament. Draw the outline of a butterfly onto waxed paper. Shave some wax crayons and arrange the shavings in a symmetrical pattern on the butterfly wings. Cover the butterfly with another piece of waxed paper. Cover with a tea towel and iron on a low heat. Cut out the butterfly. Put a piece of string at the top and hang near a window.
- Make a bird feeder. Tie string to a large pinecone. Mix together some birdseed, oats and lard. Roll the pinecone in the mix and hang from a branch near a window where you can watch the birds feeding.
- Sing this song to the tune 'He's got the whole world in his hands': we've got the whole world in our hands, we've got the whole wide world in our hands, we've got the whole world in our hands, we've got the whole world in our hands. Do hand actions making the shape of a globe and then opening the palms. Sing extra verses, for example, we've got all the wild creatures, or we've got the trees and the flowers in our hands.